MW01243406

Disclaimer

The edges of this book, not unlike the edges of a perfectly crafted chip, are not so perfect. Amazon prints each book... "uniquely." Meaning, each copy has happy accidents you can call your own.

We hope you can be patient with us on our journey towards facilitation world domination. Importantly, we hope you enjoy this book. Thank you for all of your support!

Your meetings are
STALE CHIPS

Johnny Saye & John Hawley

STALE CHIPS

Stale Chips: Innovation, Strategy & Facilitation
2022

Prelude

Meetings. (Heavy sigh). Why do they all have to be so... soul-suckingly horrid?

Well, my friend, they in fact... do not.

In this crunchy-delicious guideline, we will review an organized series of tools and tactics to **take your meetings and give them meaning.** Use this kit to help prep, facilitate, organize, and overhaul meetings for any number of people: from 1-on-1 conversations to packed auditoriums.

Conversations need structure. They benefit from a process. This booklet will help you establish simple processes derived from our experiences and failures through thousands of encounters and engagements.

First step is admitting:

Your meetings suck.
Now, let's get to learning.

Warning

Prepare for effective meetings with side effects including: free time, a happy boss, better decision-making, laughter at work.

About US

John Hawley

Father, Facilitator,
Exploratory Guide into the Possible

John can juggle and ride a unicycle at the same time. He can sing the French National Anthem in French, but has no idea what he's actually saying.

He's run over 500 workshops and developed the premier problem-solving and strategy course for the US Navy and Marine Corps. Originally the illuminate Thinkshops, it is now the curriculum for the Centers for Adaptive Warfighting (CAW). John has run offsites and retreats for the Governor of Virginia, 4-Star Admirals and Generals, and even a workshop for Billy Zane.

Johnny Saye

Dancer, Facilitator,
Ideation Obsessed Innovator

Johnny is a former professional soccer player, journalist, and vodka salesman turned innovation consultant.

He's run over 500 workshops, teaming up to create everything from juice packaging and beauty products -- to the "Uber of Security" and new forms of bioplastic. A professor of entrepreneurial strategy, author, and incredible dancer, Johnny loves to help others get further, faster.

The authors of this book created tear-evoking videos as personal "hellos." If you like weird, Goofy-movie-esque narration...

scan this code & 'meet' John and Johnny!

How to navigate

This guide is divided into a series of chapters according to various situations. You don't need to read every page, but you can! Jump directly to the Chapter highlighting your concern, and take the first step towards a meeting that matters.

Whether you use the tools in this guide yourself, provide them to your leadership team, or present them as a resource to your teammates, **you're going to begin having better meetings!**

Check the side of the guide for a quick **color find.**

Common meeting problems

Have you been caught in
any of these situations?

- Meeting finishes late (never on time or EARLY)

- It could've been an email. 100% pointless!

- Crowding out the voices of others.

- It's a dead zone: No one is speaking or responding... just a room full of Zoombies.

- No one is paying attention (looking at the "phone-focused" individuals).

- Distraction: You've got a room full of cats and a laser-pointer disco ball. A cat-astrophe.

- The meeting ends... now what? No agreed upon next steps or follow-through.

- Meetings to prepare for other meetings that wind up leading to more meetings.

How can I convince people to try this?

It's easy. The proof is in the puddin'. Well, in this case, the proof is in the corporations that have employed these methods to build products, processes, fundamentally change the way they communicate, and most importantly... **MEET!**

Ask yourself, "if the overwhelming majority of Fortune 50 companies are using it, is there something there to emulate?

You don't need to be the credibility behind trying something new with your company. All you need to do is point to the success of others. This will help with buy-in and engagement when you try to melt their minds.

IBM

THE HOME DEPOT

amazon

Google

citibank

Walmart

Edward Jones

Shell

Chapters

Chapter 1

Crunchy
Meeting Template

- ☑ 1
- ☐ 2
- ☐ 3

Unless you just want more of the same, do not start your next meeting without an incredibly quick, easy, and efficient process. Before stepping in the room, before you get a whiff of the freshly started projector and stale coffee, and before you waste anyone's time... complete the piece below.

Does this sound familiar?

You spend more time in meetings slouched over, suffering from the extreme depths of boredom, than you do from contributing meaningful work.

Why did I even get invited to this? And why, for the last 23 minutes 44 seconds, has Robert been discussing his new cat?

You're losing valuable time.
You're losing your patience.
You're about to lose your mind.

At least that's what it looks like in a lot of organizations. Simply put, **this framework transforms meetings.** You can apply it to almost any setting and in almost any group. It has **3 sections, and only 5 rules.** It also conveniently fits into the format of an email. Fill it in, send it out, and watch how quickly your meetings go from "eeeeeeew... to weeeeeee!" (scientific terms)

→ *Lazy? Explore **stalechips.com** for a template!*

Meeting: Objective

Why are you calling this meeting?

What problem or issue do you intend to discuss?

If there are multiple, please list them in order of priority. Pause before the meeting for voting to establish the topic order. During the meeting, you should come to a resolution **BEFORE** moving on to another topic.

Desired Outcomes:

If this meeting goes perfectly, what do you hope to achieve?

What does success look like?

List your goals for this meeting in short and simple tweet-like terms (280 characters for any Boomers out there). No stories or long paragraphs that nobody will even read -- just a list.

Attendees:

Who can provide value to help you reach your objective and desired outcomes? Who needs to actively contribute in the discussion? Who will be upset they were not invited? For those individuals, it's best to inform them of your actions in order to keep the team from a meltdown.

List all attendees and the role they will play in the meeting or the value you expect to get from having each of them there. Add details, documents, or pre-work needed from each individual attendee.

---Be wary to differentiate those who can contribute with those who need to be informed. CC all of those who need to be informed and clarify in your email: if you are in the CC-line, we will keep you informed of our progress, but it is not necessary for you to attend this meeting. Inevitably, you will get some uninvited guests. Don't sweat it - but don't fall witness to a meeting hijack!

Rules for all Meetings:

It's helpful to add the rules of engagement to every email with a quick refresher slide on hand during meetings.

You can easily conclude your email with, "Please see below my signature line to review meeting rules we will be observing tomorrow."

1. Only the people that need to be in the room will attend. Think of each person as a dollar figure. Is this morning chat with the company worth $20,000?

2. Everyone leaves with an aligned understanding of the defined action items.

3. Each meeting provides these specific action items tied to specific individuals.

4. This meeting will not lead to a series of follow-up meetings with no progress.

5. While you may estimate the time it will take for the meeting, we will only meet as long as necessary. If an issue is resolved in 7 minutes, the meeting will adjourn.

Chapter 2

↪

Who's in the room?

Jean

People aren't perfect, but we want to be in our meetings. To do so, we need to be able to identify and manage the varying personalities and communication styles in the room. Think of Frederick, who ALWAYS talks too much. Of Sandra, who shoots down ALL ideas. If your name is Frederick or Sandra, just pretend it says something else... We love you!

This is a game of chess. We need to strategize our victory [success]. This chapter is your guide to recognizing "who is in the room", understanding their personality, and providing tactics for getting the most out of the group.

How does it work?

Taking a page from the world of product design and marketing, we will employ Personas. What is a Persona? While each human is different, we follow certain patterns. A Persona is a fictional character we create based on research/knowledge that represents those common behaviors, needs, or desires of similar individuals. Using Personas will help us supercharge our efforts towards understanding and solving complex problems.

Note - these are meant to be exaggerated, so take no offense if you find yourself to be one of these Personas.

Don't take it persona-ly!

Shy Sam

Characteristics:

Tends to sit near people they know, often at the corner seat farthest from the Presentation Screen. Speaks only when directly spoken to and sometimes avoids eye contact. Their worst nightmare is having to stand up in front of the group.

How to conquer it:

1. Speak with "Shy Sam" prior to the meeting [or ask them something via email]. During the meeting, bring up your conversation with "Shy Sam" to the group. This will introduce them into the meeting without putting anyone on the spot.

2. Ask "Shy Sam" a question that is simple to answer and unrelated to the topic. This will give them confidence from the start.

3. Start a conversation, asking for their opinion on the topic at hand. As they respond, increase your physical distance while continuing to listen to their response. As you get farther away, they will speak a bit louder and louder until they end up speaking loud enough for the entire group to hear.

4. Give positive confirmation when they share something. Make sure to comment something like ~ "I really appreciate you sharing that. Wonderful job." Cheesy, yes, but it genuinely makes a difference!

Seasoned Susan

↓

Characteristics:

Has been an employee "since the beginning" or close to it. Tends to say, "We've tried that before". Doesn't like to try new things without poking holes in the plan, which might be disguised as their desire to be perfect. Difficult to distinguish between their hard work ethic and their intrusive nature.

How to conquer it:

1. Explain the importance of timing new ideas. In the late 1990s, a startup was raking in MILLIONS for their novel idea: Deliver groceries direct to your home via internet orders. By 2001, Webvan had filed bankruptcy. As of 2021, a direct home delivery grocery app, InstaCart, is worth $30 Billion. Right idea, wrong time.

2. Hit the "I believe button!" - Ask them to trust in the process. A process where some in the room will feel lost at first. Let "Seasoned Susan" know, like a 90's rom-com, in the end... it'll all come together.

3. Keep "Seasoned Susan" engaged by asking for insights into how it went wrong in the past or how we can prevent this new initiative from failing as it once did before. "Seasoned Susan's" perspective is EXTREMELY valuable.

4. A "Seasoned Susan" loves to poke holes in a concept, so give them that power. Assign them the role of devil's advocate and use their super strength for good!

Bossy Boss

Characteristics:

Runs the show; likes every decision to be their own. Out of passion, they will influence the thoughts of the group at any opportunity. One gaze from the Boss and the group's sharing can dry up instantly. They often have solid ideas, which could be greatly enhanced by hearing insights from others.

How to conquer it:

1. Divide and conquer. If a boss is controlling the room too much, break the group into pairs. This will limit the influence of the boss to only 1 person.

2. Before the meeting, establish an understanding of the Boss's role during the meeting by scheduling a conversation with them.

3. Call them out early! Again, this is best if discussed and planned beforehand. Plan with the boss to call them out for speaking too much, or not following the meeting rules. This will set the standard that we're all valuable during the ideation stage.

4. Ask them to skip out on the meeting until a predetermined time.

Engineer Brain

↓

Characteristics:

Logic rules everything. Feeling out of sorts or unfamiliar with a process drives them crazy; often so frustrated they end up silent-yelling like Milton from Office Space. They need order, a designated series of steps, and a reason behind everything before they commit to opening up their mind to opportunity.

How to conquer it:

1. Explain the process we are going through was established by Stanford, Google, and IBM. These "namedrops" will serve as some initial credibility.

2. Provide a loose agenda to be reviewed at the outset of the meeting. This will provide some additional security to "Engineer Brain".

3. Find a way to show outcomes early on. These outcomes will lead to their buy-in.

4. Prepare to timebox the participants. Engineers like to work until the product is at 100% completion. Timeboxing will help you establish when you've reached "good enough". Again, you've already provided the outcomes of the meeting, so your "good enough" should align very well with that.

OverSharer

↓

Characteristics:

Could be nerves -- could just be a talker. Regardless, they are eating up valuable meeting time and draining everyone's focus. Don't let them ZAP all the energy from the room!

How to conquer it:

1. At the outset of the session, let the group know you will be a stickler for time. Not to be annoying, but to get through the meeting on time or early!

2. Establish a time limit for sharing from the beginning. "During this section, each person will have 1.5 minutes to share their ideas in order to give everyone else the same opportunity to share".

3. Make it audible! If you've established a time, bring your favorite horn or download the airhorn app. Consider this auditory cue for exciting and informing the group.

4. Have a phone or access to Youtube? Start a timer and put it on the projector where all can see it. If they are speaking on a mutually interesting point, pause the timer and allow them to finish - assuming their discussion is aligned with your agenda and/or outcomes.

Do it your way!

If you find other 'Personas' popping up in your meeting frequently, feel free to create your own. Using the template shown, respond to the prompts and fill in the grid. A 'Persona' allows you to have a toolkit of tactics to keep all participants in the room engaged and productive. Before long, you won't need to reflect on them during meetings because you'll know exactly what to do!

Do you have someone attending that we didn't mention? Well, feel free to write your own Persona of this person and email it to **Crunchy@StaleChips.com.**

We can help you figure out how to conquer it!

- Persona -
Create your own

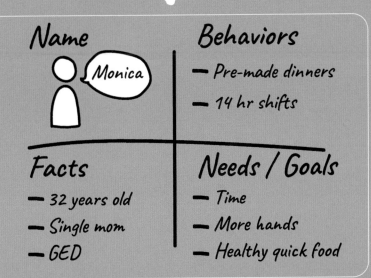

Name
Behaviors

Facts
Needs / Goals

Name
Behaviors
— Pre-made dinners
— 14 hr shifts

Monica

Facts
— 32 years old
— Single mom
— GED

Needs / Goals
— Time
— More hands
— Healthy quick food

Chapter 3

Questions before Commitment

No more shots in the dark that lead to shots to the heart. Sounds like a bad song, but don't tune out. Have you ever found yourself flailing around, racking your brain, and trying to guess what your boss wants you to create? Maybe you find yourself in a cycle like this one:

Boss says a general statement of desire. You and the team run off, create an idea. Boss rejects it. Cycle repeats 12 times. You begin losing hair from stress. Boss reviews all ideas and accepts the initial one. Ughhhhhhhh (sad face emoji). A weird mix of joy and frustration: joystration.

We've all been in this cycle of Adult Whack-a-Mole. You're not a *Psychic* and this process is *Psycho*. Let's avoid it entirely. The most important step we can take is our first, because it determines the momentum we build. Lucky for us, the world of sales and consulting have mastered the art of discovery: targeted questioning that helps us understand the needs/desires of the person we are focusing on: the user.

This will certainly take some clever maneuvering, but you're a clever individual. We're confident you can use this Chapter to shoulder the brunt of the awkwardness and put an end to finding the right color rock!

Much like the Pre-meeting template for yourself, this section is to be used immediately upon learning of a project. In just 10 questions, directed at your boss (the person assigning the task), you will learn ALL you need to create a Crunchy Meeting. Grab a piece of paper or print off our template, Mr./Ms. Efficiency. Meeting with the person who created the project/task, ask these questions in the order they are listed _ _ _ →

What are meaningful questions to ask at the start of a project?

1. What is the objective of this project?

2. What are we trying to deliver? A PPT, product, paper or presentation?

3. How will we know it was successful?

4. Who are we trying to help?

5. Who should we talk to about it?

6. What is the timeline for this project? When is it due?

7. Has this been done before? If so, what was the result?

8. If we didn't do this project, what would happen?

9. What might get in the way?

10. What other questions would help me with this project?

Chapter 4

Prioritizing:
Defining a focus

> "A wealth of information creates a poverty of attention."
> Herbet A. Simon

In several chapters of this booklet, we encourage wild and unadulterated thinking. However, we cannot overstate the importance of refining your vision. In reality, your resources are not unlimited and neither is your attention or time.

We need to limit our gaze and cut down our options.

Concentrate and create.

We answer the right questions, but find ourselves drowning in choices like an oversized restaurant menu. Then we get stuck. Options are a wonderful issue WHEN you have the tools necessary to prioritize. Without them, we end up debating, talking in endless circles, using tons of energy -- but we don't get ANYWHERE. Movement does not equal progress.

Use the following tools when you find yourself or your team in one of the following sticky situations:

- *Focusing the conversation*
- *Selecting a pathway forward*
- *Getting consensus from the group*
- *Aligning the team*

Disclaimer:

The following exercises can be completed both in-person or at *stalechips.com*.

- Vote the Note -

Share   Cluster

Vote!!!

What is it?

It's a repeatable process for groups of 3-10. It will help everyone interactively discuss and define a focus. One of the strengths of Vote the Note is the speed to arrive at a consensus. The minimal materials required is another: Sharpies, Post-its, and Dot Stickers.

How to use it?

1. Attendees have 3-4 minutes to write down ALL of their ideas or concerns on a topic.

2. ONE IDEA per Post-it. 15 words or less. Pictures welcome!

3. Each person shares ALL of their ideas, placing concepts on the board one at a time. Time-box this portion!

4. If an idea repeats, place similar ideas together, creating a cluster.

5. Continue until all participants have shared all concepts.

6. Give an equal number of stickers to all participants. These will be used as votes. This is meant to attribute the same weight per idea to each person.

For best practice

If there are less than 4 people in the meeting, give each participant 5 stickers. If greater than 4 people, give each 3.

$\overset{o}{0} < 4$ ☐☐☐☐☐

$\overset{o}{0} > 4$ ☐☐☐

When to use it?

This is your Swiss Army knife. No, I don't mean it is for carving hearts into tree trunks. Just like a Swiss Army knife, this process is extremely flexible in application. It can be used before, during, and after the meeting. At the beginning to narrow a topic, in the middle for brainstorming, and at the end for next steps.

We tend to use Vote the Note, or something similar, in almost every meeting we have: mainly to focus the group and prevent aimless discussions. Something to get all opinions out in the open. Think of this as getting a non-biased pulse before starting! From there you might be able to use your Personas (Chapter 2) to ensure these original viewpoints are not overcome by various personalities. Conversations desperately need structure and Vote the Note is the wine opener on your pocket knife that pops the cork on your conversation! (Way too committed to the knife analogy. Just go with it)

- Priori-trees -

Less More → Add Post-its More Le

What is it?

A cheesy visual pun that will save you and your group hours of time worrying about how to prioritize: problems, ideas, projects, features, outfits, ingredients (I could go ALL day!)... Using the concept of a Tree to visually organize our thoughts and structure our conversation, Priori-trees will keep you from barking up the wrong...um... Tree!

After noting all ideas, we will organize similar thoughts into "branches". The higher the priority, the closer they will get placed to the trunk of the tree.

How to use it?

1. Draw a tree similar to the sketch shown. Start with 3 branches; you can add more later if you'd like. Draw the tree large enough for your audience:

$0<5$ ⬍ $0<10$ ⬍

2. Provide 3-4 minutes to write down ALL ideas or concerns on a topic. This can be passive -- compiled in their Post-it note stack.

3. ONE IDEA per Post-it. 15 words or less. Pictures welcome!

4. Use your Priori-Tree template to help the group organize their thoughts.

5. All participants share their concepts, one at a time, placing them on a branch; closer to or farther from the trunk according to their "importance". Limit sharing each idea to 5-7 seconds.

6. Each participant needs to have an opportunity to share all their Post-its. It's best to form a line so the same person doesn't share more than one at a time.

7. If multiple ideas revolve around a similar focus, create and title a "branch" with that general topic.

8. Within each branch, organize the Post-its in order of priority, with higher priority items residing closer to the "Trunk".

9. "SHAKE the TREE". If there are any ideas that aren't needed, are EXACTLY the same, or simply out of place, allow participants to remove them from the Priori-Tree and place them at the forest floor for reference if desired.

10. In the end, clusters of leaves (Post-its) will be on a titled twig, which will all be placed on a larger titled branch. Or -- Draw the trunk-only in the beginning. Then, depending on clusters, you can name each branch.

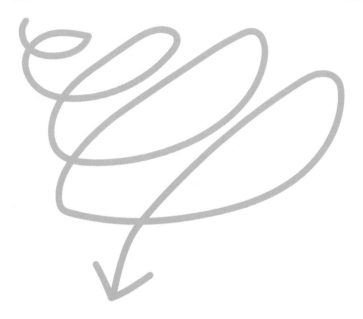

When to use it?

Anytime you need to get a quick roadmap or alignment of the way ahead. While coaching a bank through a new App, we used the Priori-Tree to define which **features** would be the most useful to their customers. In a less technical setting, we like to use this before laying out a **strategy** for a business or project. It provides a structure for getting the group on the same page, getting a FULL view of the tasks being taken on, and providing a short roadmap for each piece of the project/ strategy.

Save the chips!
The Bake and Shake:

1. Sprint (carefully) into the kitchen and turn your oven to 400 degrees F.

2. Patiently wait for the preheat to complete.

3. Gracefully pour the bag of chips onto a cooking tray. Leave space for each to get crunchy.

4. Allow for 2 minutes of crisping time.

5. Celebrate... because you just put some crunch back in your lunch (or dinner)!

- Knockout! -

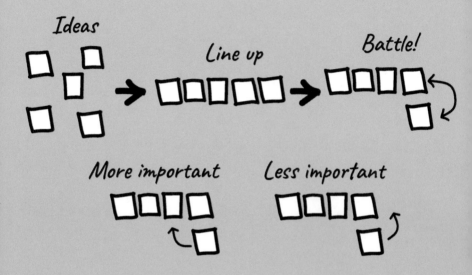

Ideas

Line up

Battle!

More important

Less important

What is it?
No punches will be thrown, ideally. Knockout is a head to head battle between all ideas. How is that possible? As the facilitator, the pressure will be on you as you walk the group through each individual idea. Be patient, be practical, and don't include more than 15 concepts.

How to use it?

1. Get the group to collectively write down the top 15 (or less) concepts of the meeting with one idea per Post-it. If you wind up with too many ideas, use voting strategies found on (Pg.26) to limit to 15.

2. Place the Post-its in a single line from right to left. Left will be our "Champions Square" -- the most important concept.

3. Before you begin, allot 45 seconds for the group to place the ideas in their best guess on the line of importance. This will save a lot of time.

4. Explain the rules: Our goal is to order all the ideas from Most to Least important (left to right). To do so, let's begin the game of Knockout.

5. As the facilitator, bring the group's attention to the first Post-it on the far right.

6. Ask which Post-it is more important: The one you have selected, or the one to it's immediate left. BOOM. Head to Head battle. Now we are in a Knockout.

7. If the FIRST Post-it (on the right) wins, move it forward one space to the left and repeat the question: Which Post-it is more important? If the Post-it loses, leave it in place and begin to compare the two to it's immediate left.

8. Continue until our original Post-it (the 'FIRST' on the right), loses. Leave it where it loses.

9. Restart back on the far right (what was originally the 2nd post-it from the right).

10. Repeat the process mentioned in Step 6.

11. Continue this process until your line represents the most important on the left to least important on the right.

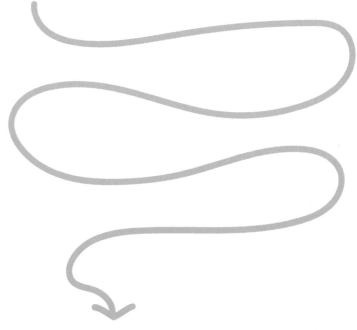

When to use it?

This can be a superpower for generating discussion after having the group individually write down all their problems or after a brainstorming session closes. It allows the group to focus exclusively on the impact/importance of just 2 ideas, as opposed to reviewing 10 ideas at once. Many individuals struggle with weighing multiple options at once and simply pick the most recent in their memory. Knockout prevents this slant in decision-making.

Save the chips!
The Speedster:

1. Locate the nearest microwave. Those day old chips still have hope!

2. Spread chips across a dry paper towel. We need to zap out some moisture.

3. High heat for 30 seconds.

4. Cautiously test 1 chip with a reasonable amount of guac.

5. Repeat the process until righteously crunchy!

Chapter 5

Problem Hunting: Search Party

We prefer to fall in love with our problems (and their intense siblings who judge you for not knowing how to fish).

What does that even mean?
To dive headfirst into a solution is to jump off a bridge without knowing the depth of the water.

We need context -- we need understanding -- we need **Problem Hunting.** We divide our process into two areas: the **Problem Space** and the **Solution Space**. We must commit to the former before the latter. To fully grasp the power of context, read through this simple riddle.

A man walks into a bar and asks the bartender for a glass of water. The bartender reaches under the bar, brings out a gun, and aims it at the man. The man says thank you and leaves. What happened?

We'll explain. The man who nearly got a handful of lead as opposed to a cupful of water -- his problem was simple; he had the hiccups. The bartender was merely hoping to help by scaring the hiccups out of the man, which he accomplished successfully. Without knowing the context, this would seem like an odd turn of events. With the proper context we can ask ourselves, "was that truly the best solution?"

The key lesson: jumping straight to the conclusion often leaves you with a one-dimensional solution. Likely one with minimal application. Don't solve the wrong problem -- Fall in love, find the context, THEN solve it!

The following exercises guide you or a group through the process of identifying and understanding a problem with no hiccups!

Sherlock, it's time to go on the hunt.

Stake-Hold on a Minute

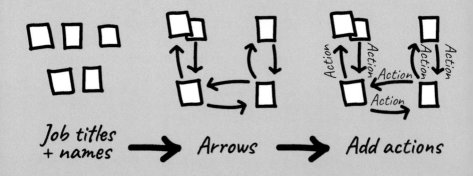

Job titles + names ➜ Arrows ➜ Add actions

What is it?

A great method for getting The Who (not the band) of a problem. Used as the first step in **Problem Hunting**, this tool paints a clear picture of individuals in our area of focus. It's impossible to complete a puzzle without looking deeply at the pieces. "Stake-Hold on a Minute" magnifies the group's ability to zoom in on those involved with the problem.

How to use it?

1. Ask the group to write down ALL stakeholders involved in or impacted by the problem. One stakeholder per Post-it.

2. Each Post-it should have a job title and a fictitious name (make it fun).

3. Participants take 3-4 minutes to write down as many as possible.

4. Place ideas on the wall. Each participant needs to have an opportunity to share all their Post-its. It's best to create a line so the same person doesn't share more than one at a time.

5. If another participant has an idea that matches, place them on or directly next to similar Post-its.

6. Repeat the process until all stakeholders are added to the board.

7. Add arrows and actions. Arrows show the interaction of one stakeholder on another. Each arrow has its own action. See sketch for clarification.

8. Add an action to each arrow. This action will describe the "interaction" of one stakeholder to another.

9. Continue adding arrows and actions between the stakeholders until all interactions are shown.

When to use it?

Start here when looking for a problem. We use this exercise with new projects or groups in order to define our current understanding of a problem, to include gaps, and get all information out on the table. We also recommend combining this exercise with Stake-Hold on a Minute #2 (Pg.40) and a Pain Rain session (Pg.46).

Stake-Hold on a Minute #2

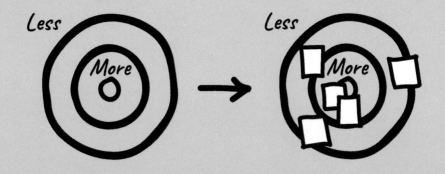

What is it?

Forming a piece of the partner package with **Stake-Hold on a Minute**, this process is about guiding our focus. Now we will look at the impact of the situation at hand as well as the interactions: Who is the most impacted by this? Target... Acquired.

How to use it?

1. Begin with the stakeholders from the previous exercise on (Pg.38). If you are starting from the beginning, ask the group to write down ALL stakeholders involved in or impacted by the problem. One stakeholder per Post-it. (Who is impacted by it? Who interacts with it?)

2. Draw a 3-ringed target similar to the sketch shown.

3. Ask the group to begin adjusting the stakeholders into their corresponding "ring", with the most impacted at the center and the least impacted on the outermost "ring".

4. If someone from the group places a Post-it on the target, they must explain the thinking behind its placement. Limit time of explanation.

5. As the facilitator, allow for discussion. If little discussion is occurring, ask simple probing questions: What's your thought process behind that placement? Is there anything we are forgetting? How does this relate to the last exercise we did? Do you agree with what's already been placed?

6. Continue placing the Post-its on the target until all relevant stakeholders are added.

7. If a stakeholder appears to be unnecessary, simply leave them off the Target or place them in a "parking lot" for deeper discussion later.

When to use it?

While the initial Stake-Hold on Minute opened up a scary wave of information, we use this exercise to control our focus. We cannot solve every problem for every person at once. Let's zoom in on the most impacted in order to work our way to the first domino. If we tip that first one over, the rest of the problems will follow. A common interpretation of this focus is known as the 80-20 rule. Solve the problem causing 80% of your issues first, then work on the more nuanced 20%.

Sailboating

What is it?

Sunscreen and honesty are needed. This is one of the EASIEST methods for identifying problems. It's not always "smooth sailing", but with a group of eager and open participants, Sailboating will navigate your ship to countless treasures! (and other marine puns)

How to use it?

1. Draw a Sailboat (no Picasso needed) similar to the sketch.

2. Use the topic of the meeting as the focus point. Example, What's going well with our department? What's holding our department back?

3. The Sailboat is separated into two sections: The Wind and the Anchor. The wind is what is propelling us forward. The anchor is what is holding us back. Wind -- positive -- solutions. Anchor -- negative -- problems.

4. Ask each participant to respond to the Wind first, giving them 3 minutes to write down as many responses to the following prompt: What is currently going well with this topic? One response per Post-it. Pictures are welcome and aim for less than 15 words.

5. As mentioned in other exercises, allow each participant to share ideas, grouping similar concepts together. This is merely a warm-up section. A feel-good moment.

6. Anchor: ask participants to write down as many responses as possible to the following prompt: What is going wrong with the current topic?

7. Everyone shares, grouping similar Post-its into clusters.

8. Voting: give each participant 3-5 dots (depending on group size). Give everyone 1 minute to mentally select their favorite problem for the group. Silently vote when ready.

9. Notice dependencies: issues that are connected like dominoes to one another.

10. Count up the votes, physically moving the Post-its from the voting section to their own clean wall. Organize according to votes.

11. Have a group discussion about the results and make any adjustments.

12. Problem Solving is next!

When to use it?

Start here when looking for the right problem to solve. We use this exercise with new projects or teams in order to define current understanding of a problem, identifying gaps, and tap into all of the information available. Consider combining this exercise with Stake- Hold on a Minute #2 (Pg.40) and a Pain Rain session (Pg.46).

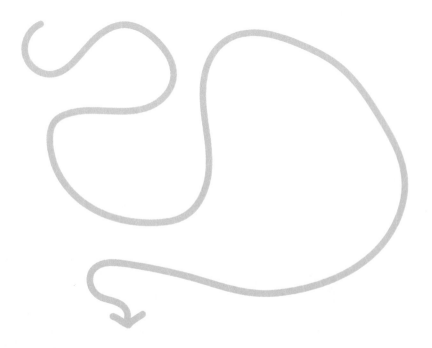

For best practice

When voting, set a limit of votes per person per a given Post-it note. This will prevent any one individual from having too much sway over the results.

Epic list of alternative uses for stale bag of chips:

Soup de Jour

Don't let that head sag from a stale bag. Give those chips a new purpose atop a wonderfully delicious soup.

Not so crumby idea

Have a food processor or a little anger and a hammer? Take the chips and quickly create an alternative to bread crumbs. Whip up some delicious fried chicken or go fancy with a pan seared grouper.

Pain Rain!

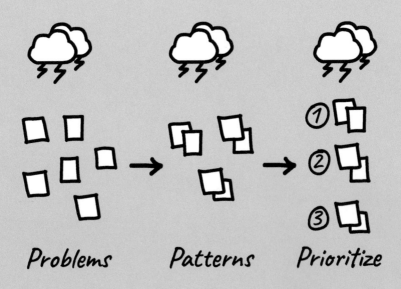

Problems   Patterns   Prioritize

What is it?

Not the purple rain of Prince, but equally beautiful. This 100% depends on the quality of the participants you have in the room. The closer to the problem they are, the better results this exercise will bring you. In less formal engagements, this is known as a "Mega Venting Seshhh". Do your work up front and find a mix of those directly impacted by the topic of discussion: Managers, Floor Workers, Drivers, Zookeepers. WHOEVER!

How to use it?

1. Give each of the participants a FAT stack of Post-its and challenge them to fill in as MANY as possible.

2. Participants write down all the problems they have with a current topic. Cheer on those who have the most.

3. Allow everyone to continue writing until a notable drop in Post-it adding occurs. Stop the rain!

4. Each participant needs to have an opportunity to share all their Post-its. It's best to form a semi-circle and select one to begin sharing.

5. If anyone else in the group has a similar pain, have them come up to the board and place it directly NEXT to the Post-it shared before moving to the next person.

6. Get clarification: "Could you tell me more about it?"

7. Stare at the wall, which is now filled with a wide array of issues this group is collectively suffering from. The larger the cluster, the bigger the red flag. It shows an obvious problem that can be seen from multiple perspectives.

8. Discuss the results with the group: Why has this problem been mentioned so often?

When to use it?

This exercise serves as a shortcut to the truth. Expertly select those to attend the workshop to have a mix of hands-on experience, leadership, rookies, and at least a couple completely unknowledgeable, but highly opinionated, individuals. This intentional mix will yield the best results. We frequently use it to get additional context to a problem before we move on to the **SOLUTION SPACE**. Plus, people love a good venting session!

⚠ **Caution:** if you are new to facilitation, take the time to establish proper ground rules to ensure it doesn't turn into a free-for-all!

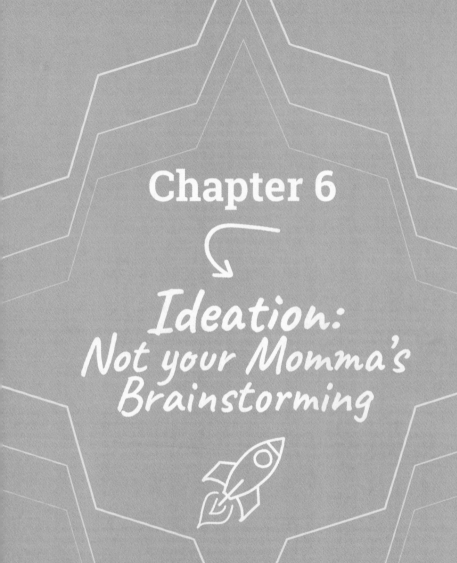

Chapter 6

Ideation:
Not your Momma's Brainstorming

Let me guess: you or someone in the meeting "isn't creative"? Highly unlikely... especially with the right tools. This is a falsehood that was repeated so many times it became true. Something we've programmed ourselves to believe. Maybe as a child, you were asked to draw in class.

To your misfortune, the person to your left happened to be Michelangelo. You said "I can't draw so I guess I'm not very creative" (you know how kids talk). Or maybe in choir you sang your heart out but stood next to Beyoncé. And so-on until you ended up believing a lie. Creativity isn't limited to art. Anyone can be creative. A lawyer in the way they defend their case or a computer engineer writing code. You can be creative. You ARE creative!

In this section, we organize the mind to explode into opportunities, pulling from a variety of methodologies with a single result: to create.

Remember, creativity is like a muscle. It takes reps and sets to grow!

Back from the Future

What is it?

Start from the end. This is not like eating dessert first. This is a common tactic for improving ideas and decision-making. We will imagine what the future (3 years time) will look like before working backwards to the present, building out the steps needed to get there. What's the benefit? By imagining the future, we allow ourselves to be more creative and free from the limitations of the current times. This will create a different perspective to tap into the tacit knowledge of the group.

How to use it?

1. Select ONE problem as the focus for the brainstorming.

2. Write the problem in large text on the wall or mural so it is easily visible.

3. Ask how we would solve this problem if we lived 100 years in the future? We are looking for wild and crazy ideas! Ensure they understand this.

4. Allow the group 3 minutes to individually and silently write as MANY ideas as possible, one idea per Post-it.

5. Each participant shares their wild ideas, while everyone else encourages and applauds the craziest. This is important to expand the creativity of the rest of the group.

6. Refocus the group by asking for responses to the following prompt: We are now 3 years in the future and we did an INCREDIBLE job solving this problem. What did we do to get here?

7. Allow the group 3 minutes to individually and silently write as MANY ideas as possible, one idea per post-it.

8. Each participant needs to have an opportunity to share all their Post-its. It's best to form a semi-circle and select one to begin sharing. Pause for comments throughout.

9. Cluster similar ideas as you go.

10. Give each participant 3-5 dot stickers for voting, asking the group to vote on the "best solution". Allow "best" to be up for interpretation or define it as a group before voting.

When to use it?

Before attacking a large project, we find this exercise to be incredibly effective. We use it to align our assumptions and initial perspectives. Additionally, it helps a group struggling through brainstorming. This will free them of any and all current limitations. "It's not possible" and "We don't have time/money" all goes out the window. For next-level facilitation: Bring a bag full of wacky sunglasses to the session. When asking the group to think of the future, let them know you have 'magic technology' which helps participants see the future. Some tech you "borrowed" from the government. Simply hand out the sunglasses and enjoy!

Zombie Alarm System

Place stale chips on floors across house. If zombie enters, instantly know. Or if you're hungry, have a snack on the go.

Brainwriting

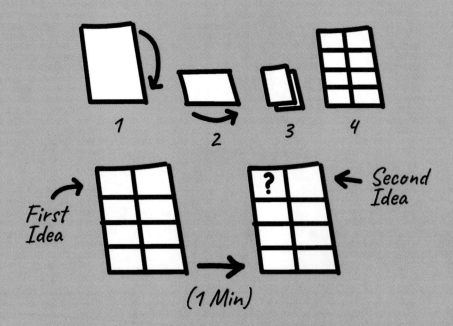

1 2 3 4

First
Idea

(1 Min)

Second
Idea

?

What is it?

A tactic for rapidly generating lots and lots of ideas by creating a time-crunch and encouraging "yes-and" thinking. "Yes-and" thinking is easy: after hearing or writing an idea, simply try to add onto that existing concept to plus it up or create something new. Do not put down the idea. Think improv! Grab paper, pens, and a stopwatch. It's time to stretch the mind!

How to use it?

1. Give each participant in the group a single sheet of standard (A4) printer paper, or check out our Mural template at **www.stalechips.com**

2. Participants fold paper to create 8 equally sized rectangles as shown in the sketch.

3. Write ONE idea in the top LEFT corner of the page.

4. Now that everyone has their starting idea, we will follow a set pattern. Participants will have 1 minute to create a new idea to the immediate right of the original idea. It can be completely new or a "yes-and" of something else.

5. After 1 minute, call TIME (place timer in location for all to see or simply use your phone).

6. At 1 minute, the participants must move to a new rectangle and repeat the process.

7. Continue until ALL 8 rectangles are full on the page with ideas.

8. Each participant picks their 3 favorite ideas, circling them after taping their sheets to the wall.

Bonus

1. For NEXT LEVEL Brainwriting, set the group up in a circle.

2. After writing their initial idea, have each participant pass their paper to the left.

3. Now participants must look at their neighbors' idea and generate a new concept using "yes-and" with only 1 minute on the clock.

4. Continue the process until ALL 8 rectangles are full or the paper returns to its owner.

When to use it?

Quantity before Quality. In this mind-stretching exercise, participants are pushed to generate ideas at high speeds. We like to use it after finding a prioritized problem. It allows for the group to step past that initial obvious solution and dig into less standard concepts.

Medici Method

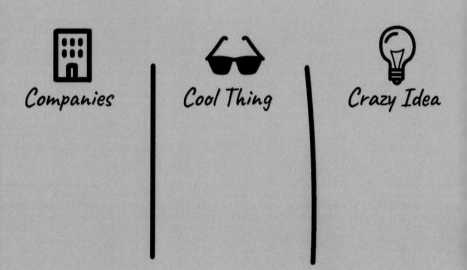

Companies | Cool Thing | Crazy Idea

What is it?

This famous family of old Florence, Italy were known for their wealth... and their sticky fingers. While we don't condone stealing, we do love being inspired by the ideas of others. With the Medici Method, we have a recipe using the special sauce of the world's best companies to create our own, sometimes similar, flavor. We don't always need to reinvent the wheel to reinvent the art of our possible.

How to use it?

1. Draw the sketch shown or download a copy of our template at **www.stalechips.com.**

2. Ask participants to name companies they think have been outperforming others. Make sure to pick outside of your industry. If you work for Ford, don't pick Toyota.

3. After sharing a company name, ask the group, "What makes this company unique? Why are they better?" Ensure you're able to get a concrete response. IE: Chick-fil-a's consistency of product and logistics of customers.

4. Fill in the first TWO COLUMNS of the template as a group.

5. Individually brainstorm, focusing on one company at a time and writing ALL ideas down on Post-its (one idea per Post-it).

6. With another company, ask, "How could we do that in our industry?" For example: How could we move customers as fast as Chick-Fil-a?

7. Give the group 7 minutes and encourage them to use their phones or laptops to do guerrilla research. Steal! I mean... borrow ideas from companies doing incredibly well and add a special spice that makes it yours.

8. Share findings and ideas.

9. Discuss which options could be the best path forward or use one of the prioritization methods (Pg.24) to select a winner!

When to use it?

As noted by Austin Kleon in **"Steal Like an Artist,"** many of the most creative people in the world are simply experts at... borrowing ideas from others and enhancing. Taking a concept from one market and moving it to another. The drone: from military use to movies. Play-Doh: from cleaning equipment to an amazing fidget toy. Finding inspiration from others and applying best practices from one industry to a new one is a fast way to fruitful ideas.

Chapter 7

↳

Action Items: What to do when you're done

You made it through a meeting and are thinking to yourself, "So what?! Three hours have passed, conversations have been had, but what tangible steps are we taking from this gathering?"

It's time to cut through the fluff and assign responsibilities. **Action Items** aren't just scribbles on a board. They are the bridge that takes us from chatting to happening, talking to walking, and saying it to displaying it.

Why are **Action Items** so vital? Meetings that lead to more meetings are the hamster wheel of adult life. Little direction, no progress, and sometimes oddly entertaining. We are determined to find progress.

This chapter will dive into using a simple template to assure your action items are easy to define, understand, and track. Completing them... well that is up to you (and your superstar team)!

It can be challenging to divy up efforts. Especially because there might not be enough time to speak with leadership. Even if you can't identify the perfect person, we will walk you through how you might be able to identify a point of contact for an action item.

Action!

☑️ To(Do) | ??? Who | 📅 Due | 🙌 Wooh!

What is it?

This template is divided into four sections: To(Do), Who, Due, and Wooh!

1. **To(Do):** What will they do?
2. **Who:** Who will do it?
3. **Due:** When does it need to be done?
4. **Wooh!:** How important is it?

The four sections are designed to be as SIMPLE and CLEAR as possible. Also, Wooh! Is the only word we could think of to rhyme with the rest.

How to use it?

1. As a group, write down a list of **"To(Do)s"** from the meeting. This can be done however you'd like: individually before discussion, or collectively as a group.

2. With the list of **"To(Do)s"** completed and added to the template, move on to the other categories.

3. Assign each **To(Do)** to a **Who**, having them read their task out loud and allow the group to ask any clarifying questions they may have. This is to assure no work is wasted because of miscommunication. Remember, you selected the people in this meeting because they mattered to these outcomes. If someone is not present, someone should still be responsible to ask or inform that individual. Assigning is best accomplished by pressuring the group to "sign-up" for the tasks that make the most sense for them to run.

4. Allow the individual to assign their own **Due-Date** with the assistance of the group.

5. Establish a **Wooh!** (importance grade) to each task. This will ensure the proper attention is given to each task in the event anything needs to be "parked" temporarily. Parked tasks don't contribute to the immediate goal. If we are trying to solve computer issues but find ourselves talking about shoes for 5 minutes, let's park the Nikes.

6. Repeat the process until all tasks are defined, assigned, timelined, and prioritined (we tried).

7. High-Five your teammates. You all have done it! A meeting that matters.

When to use it?

In order to create real progress we need more than basic meetings. We need the meat and potatoes. The action items created during the meeting will cement the results of the conversations and decisions made by the group. In other words, it's an agreement. At the end of EVERY meeting, we use this simple format to build out our path forward and create a system of accountability.

What's

next?

Chapter 8

Conclusions

Ah, you crunch master flex. You've made it to the final chapter (or... simply opened the book randomly to this page). But we don't want you to leave thinking you can conquer the world with these tools. The magic isn't in the tool, yourself, or even in us (surprising, we know). The magic is in intentional focus on effective communication. And by golly, I think you might have it!

Now you're ready to run an entire 6 hour workshop all by yourself! Look at me... in the eyes. **DO NOT DO THAT.** Take it one tool at a time. Test out making a decision as a group with Vote the Note, learn to cross oceans of concern with Sailboating, save millions coming Back from the Future. Listen more than you speak, learn more than you teach, and if you find yourself hungry for more... check out these amazing resources

Sessionslab:

If you want to see what else the world has to offer, and still have a little hand-holding... this is for you. A wide variety of completely planned out workshops, simple tools, and tried/true tactics to conquer your communication.

Board of Innovation:

Smooth like the back of the spoon, these are the cool kids of innovation and they are pumping out some massively crunchy online resources around trends, tools, and new ideas. Use these peeps to find the cutting edge of... "Hey, that's pretty neat."

Boardle.io:

This is your lifeline for creating online workshops in a matter of clicks. Experts from around the world curate and build their own templates... kindly giving you free access for world domination, or better decision-making for your team.

Stale Chips:

A dedicated team of people nerds who are wholeheartedly in love with problem-solving, Stale Chips is a source for all things innovation, strategy and facilitation. Whether it be a course, a quick article, or world-famous podcast "Crunch Time w/ Stale Chips," we're there for every step of the learning experience.

Before, you found your meetings to be a lot like 2020: chaotic, complex, and claustrophobic. Now (wipes tears of joy), you have done it. You incredible and amazing meeting maestro! But with great wisdom comes even greater meeting responsibility. Take this knowledge, these tactics, and share them.

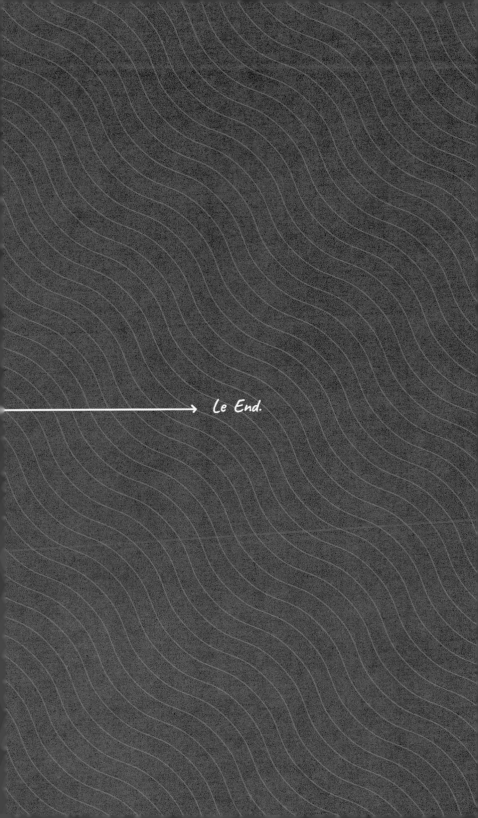

→ *Le End.*

Don't like reading?
Then watch it!

Well, it's not too late (if you're reading this book backwards). It's never too late.

While this book gives you the inside scoop to improving meetings, it's just a start.

We've created a series of 9 courses to cover all your meeting musts: from an extensive toolkit to full-on facilitation tactics, these slices of info-tainment are designed to help you get the most out of any team and solve any problem.

Innovation, Strategy, & Facilitation.
Come get crunchy with us at Stale Chips School.

Stale Chips
School

Helping teams get further, faster.

STALE CHIPS

We gave you our .02 cents. Could you give us yours? To keep
improving and spreading the word, a review on Amazon goes a long
way. Stay crunchy!

Made in the USA
Middletown, DE
23 September 2023